Hardwood • Vinyl • Lan

FLOORING
BASICS

√ **SELECTING**   √ **ESTIMATING**

√ **PREPARING**   √ **INSTALLING**

Chip Alliman

CONTENTS

Introduction

Hardwood flooring is one of the most important assets in any home. Not only do new floors add value to your home from a financial point of view, they also add value in the overall warmth and appeal of your home.

In a survey of real estate agents across our country, 90 percent agreed that "houses with wood flooring sell faster and for higher prices than houses without wood floors."

Hardwood, vinyl, and laminate floors are becoming more popular because they are ecologically friendly. This renewable resource helps your home stay free of allergens to provide you with a health-friendly environment for your growing family.

Not only is cleaning and maintenance made easier with today's finishes, but the hardwood look is timeless and can last the life of your home.

This book is directed specifically at what is referred to as pre-finished flooring. You'll find information about selecting the right products for your home. More importantly, this book with help you better understand all of the processes involved in the installation of your hardwood, vinyl, or laminate flooring. We'll also give you information on the maintenance and care for the variety of floor finishes that are available today.

Hardwood, vinyl, or laminate flooring is like so many successful home projects in that it must begin with good planning and set up. A smart plan to get you started on the project right will pay off in the end result.

We urge you to read each chapter carefully and thoroughly, underlining and marking key points that will be applicable to your project.

We're assuming you are pretty handy and already have some of the basic tools required for general household repairs. Tools like pry bars, nail sets, and chalk lines are just a few of the hand tools necessary for flooring installation.

Let's begin!

PART I — SELECTING

Selecting the correct pre-finished flooring must begin by an understanding of the terms above grade, on grade, and below grade. To properly make this judgement you must begin by looking at your home, the lot it is on, its relationship to the surrounding landscape, and how heavy rains and water runoff impact the various levels of your home.

Above or Below Grade?

First, you must determine where in your home the flooring will be installed. Looking at the following examples will give you a good view of what must be considered for

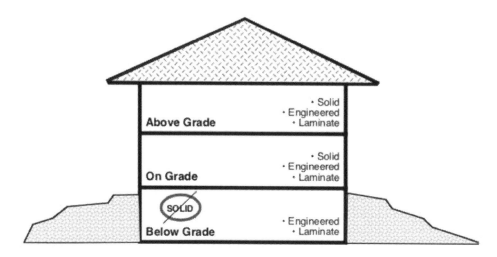

your project and hardwood selection. Installations below grade have to contend with moisture or at least the possibility of moisture. It is natural for moisure to be present in the soil surrounding the building and transferring that moisure through the concrete or wood foundation.

Due to the fabrication of engineered flooring moisture is less likely to have a dramatic shrinkage or swelling effect on the product. This is possible due to the construction which allows the different materials to equalize as moisture is pulled in.

In the case of laminates the flooring is comprised of glues and non-wood components pressed together to form the finished product, then imprinted with an image of the selected wood grain on the suface.

Most products, pre-finished, engineered and laminate, can be floated over concreate surfaces. The strips are glued or "clicked" together, but are normally not connected directly to the concrete. For below grade installation this is our recommendation for the do-it-yourself consumer.

For on grade or above grade installation all types of prefinished flooring can be used with great success. Each specific flooring manufacturer will have specific guidelines for installing their product, but the following is what we would consider acceptable installations in the order of their user friendliness.

Easy - Laminate Flooring

A floating installation with a self-locking tongue and groove would be considered the easiest flooring to install. The process is quick and fairly easy.

Medium-Engineered (Floating) & Engineered (Staple-Down)

Engineered hardwood offers an option in installation with either a floating, self-locking tongue and groove type or a standard staple-down type if you are installing over an existing plywood subfloor. Both of these installations offer a real wood look since the top layer is usually made of solid wood. This also offers you the option to apply fresh top coats of urethane to maintain the sheen and protect the product.

Medium/Hard - 5/16" up to 3/4" Standard Strip Solid Hardwood

There are now numerous brands of standard full 3/4 inch solid hardwood products on the market. We consider this to be a little more than medium in difficulty since it will require more consideration for acclimation and you can expect it to shrink and expand with the seasons like sanded and finished hardwood flooring.

PART II — ESTIMATING & QUANTITIES

Measuring, Estimating, & Determining Square Footage

Once you have selected the type and desired look for your new hardwood floors, it's time to begin compiling your materials list for the project. The first step is to measure your rooms and areas and calculate the square footage of hardwood that you will need.

Nearly all prefinished hardwood will come in boxes that contain about twenty square feet. It is very important that you read carefully the instructions that will come in the boxes of your selected flooring. These are generally very specific as to the importance of a level floor for installation. Many manufacturers tend to be very demanding in requirements like this, since it will play a major role if you end up with any kind of warranty claim.

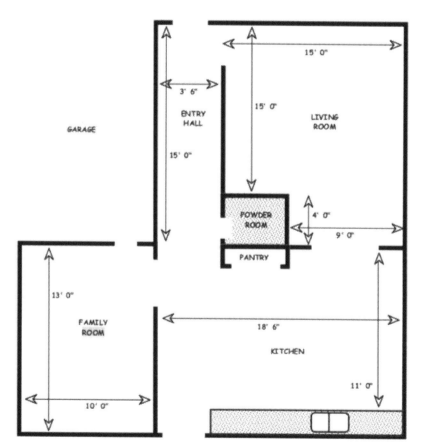

Our layout is not to scale, but it will give you a good idea of how square footage is measured and calculated, so let's do some measuring.

Based on our plan we list the measurements as follows. Note that 6 inches is one-half of a foot, therefore to multiply you use .5 for one-half.

Entry	3.5	x	150	=	52.5
Living Room	15.0	x	15.0	=	225.0
	9.0	x	4.0	=	36.0
Kitchen	18.5	x	11.0	=	203.5
Family Room	10.0	x	13.0	-	130.0

647.0

Our project area total is 647 square feet.

When ordering you must also calculate for waste, then take into consideration how many square feet come in each box of hardwood. Waste factor is also determined by the percentage of area in your project made up of halls, closets, angles, and the like that tend to consume more waste. It is always a good idea to have extra product remaining at the end of any project. A water leak, spilled chemical, or dropped tool can require some replacement at a future date.

Using a waste factor formula of 10%, our final total of needed hardwood is:

647.0
x   1.10

Hardwood needed for the project ....**712.0 square feet**

For our example, let's assume the hardwood we selected comes in boxes with 21.5 square feet per box. We divide 712.0 by 21.5 and get 33.12. In this case, we would order 33 boxes of hardwood since the .12 overage is marginal. Of course, there are other items that will need to be included in our materials order.

Nosing and Reducers

There might, for example, be a step down from the kitchen to the family room. If that is the case, you will need to install a piece of bullnose at the edge of that step down.

Many pre-finished products have matching reducers available in lengths of about six feet. On the following pages you will find samples of reducers and their application. With some of the very thin pre-finished products on the market, care should be given with reducers. Gluing reducers firmly to the floor will help to reduce the possibility of damage and breakage especially in heavy traffic areas.

Quarter-Round

Quarter-round is used at the base of cabinets in kitchens, baths, and utility rooms. Since there is usually a slight variation in the space where hardwood butts up to the bottom of a cabinet, installing a piece of quarter-round, stained and finished to match, will give you a nice finished look.

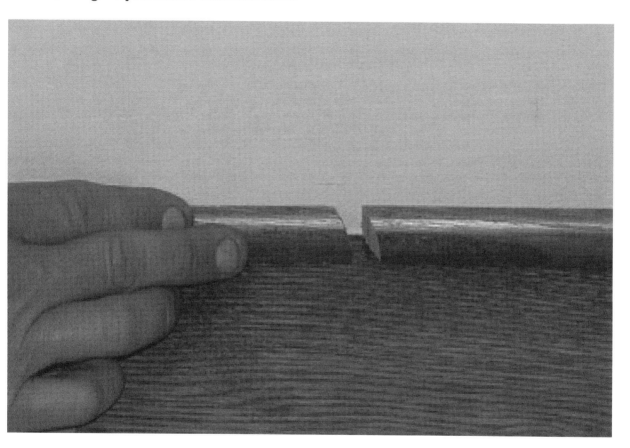

Cutting an angle at a connecting joint will help hide the joint and give a more finished look.

Quarter-round comes in a variety of widths and styles, and most manufacturers offer it along with their reducers and transition strips.

For a more finished look on corners and seams, it is best to cut the joining pieces at angles to help hide the joints. The photo on page 11 will help you visualize that kind of cut.

Pre-Finished transition strips normally come in about 6 ft. lengths to match the pre-finished flooring. On the left is a "T-Mold" that is used to connect the hardwood to other flooring such as the tile shown here.

Glues

If glue is to be used in the project, most hardwood manufacturers will require that you use their recommended glue in order to come under their warranty. Again, we strongly urge you to read their installation instructions carefully to be sure you are applying the glue in the recommended places, in the recommended amounts.

Measurement Checklist

Area	Width	x	Depth	=	Total
_____	_____	x	_____	=	_____
_____	_____	x	_____	=	_____
_____	_____	x	_____	=	_____
_____	_____	x	_____	=	_____
_____	_____	x	_____	=	_____
_____	_____	x	_____	=	_____
_____	_____	x	_____	=	_____
_____	_____	x	_____	=	_____
_____	_____	x	_____	=	_____
_____	_____	x	_____	=	_____
_____	_____	x	_____	=	_____
_____	_____	x	_____	=	_____
_____	_____	x	_____	=	_____
_____	_____	x	_____	=	_____
_____	_____	x	_____	=	_____

Total s.f. _____

Waste x 1.10

Hardwood needed for project _____

My selection comes _____ s.f. per box

I need to order _____ boxes

Materials to Order

Product: Brand   _____

                Name   _____

                Color   _____

Product	Square Footage Needed	_____
Nosing	Linear Feet	_____
Reducer/T-Mold	Linear Feet	_____
Quarter-round	Linear Feet	_____
Glue	Amount Needed	_____
Foam	For Floating Floors	_____
Tape	For Foam Seams	_____
Putty	Color to match	_____
Underlayment	(If Recommended)	_____

Removing Stools & Pedestal Sinks

After more than three decades in the flooring and construction industry, this issue could be reduced to one sentence — "Call a plumber!" Removing those items is not difficult, but reinstalling them once your flooring is in place can be risky. Professional help can save you a good deal of disappointment and additional costs.

Removing Baseboard

Removing the baseboards is required before installation can begin. A utility knife, a wide chisel, a pry bar, and a hammer should be all you need to remove baseboards in the project area. It is important that you run your new flooring close to the wall at each end so the slightly staggered ends will be covered when you replace the baseboard.

Most baseboard has been installed with staples or finish nails and will pry off easily. Don't underestimate the importance of running a cut line at the top of the baseboard where it lays against the wall. Whether it was caulked, painted, or if there is

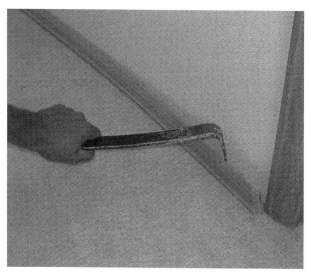

wallpaper on the wall behind it, running that cut line will save you time and frustration. The cut line assures separation when the baseboard is pried from the wall, it does not bring anything with it that is attached to the wall. Follow the photo as you carefully tap the pry bar about an inch or so deep behind the baseboard at one end, then pry slowly to see if it will come loose easily. If it will, gradually work your way along that piece of baseboard until it is removed.

Warning: When you pry be careful that you don't let the chisel or pry bar have so much leverage that it sinks into the drywall behind the baseboard. This indentation will show later when you reset the baseboard. The best tool is a pry bar like you see in the photo. As you can see, inserting the short end of the pry bar, then **lightly moving it to the right or left** (rather than up or down) will allow good leverage to loosen the baseboard.

Once the board is removed, be sure you number the back of that baseboard piece, putting the same number near the floor on the wall where you removed it.

This is also a good time to clean up your baseboard. A new coat of paint will do wonders for scuffed baseboard and compliment your new flooring. If your baseboard is stained, find a stain that is close in color and, using a rag, wipe a new coat onto the baseboard. If you're really energetic you can brush on a coat of urethane also.

Removing Carpet

Removing carpet will take time and labor. As we noted, the easiest way to remove carpet is with a sharp, carpet knife. Cut the carpet across the room into strips about four feet wide by six to eight feet long. Roll these strips up, wrap them with twine, and dispose of them. Do the same with the carpet pad, although it is often held in place with numerous staples that have to be plucked one-by-one. The tack strips around the edges also have to be pried up. Make certain all nails are removed.

Removing Tile, Vinyl, and Linoleum

In most cases tile, vinyl, and linoleum will have an underlayment under it. This is normally a sheet of plywood about 1/8" thick. It might be tacked or glued in.

It is important that you remove everything until you're down to the original subfloor. Stripping everything will assure you a level connection from one area to the next in your home without transition strips which can catch a toe or snag a sock.

In some older homes mastic glues were used to hold linoleum in place. These can be difficult to get up and may require a labor-intensive scraping of the area to get it to level and smooth. Doing a thorough job will pay dividends later.

Inspecting The Subfloor

Now is a good time to carefully inspect the subfloor. Walk it slowly looking for squeaks, nail heads, and loose or rotted boards. Often floors squeak because of the wood-on-wood where the subfloor is nailed to the joists below it. If this is the case drive a few deck screws into those boards to eliminate all movement.

Carefully inspect for rotted boards, if you find a damaged area now is the best time to replace it to stabilize your subfloor. Since you can't see under the subfloor, carefully nail or screw it into the joists. There is always the possibility of a water pipe or electrical wiring running under the subfloor. It is wise to spend some time in your basement or crawl space looking for anything that could cause problems.

Check For Level

Most manufacturers are sticklers about level floors and their warranty. Some go beyond reason, but the more level the floor the better the finished product in both looks and durability. If you have a long straight edge lay it across the floor in various areas and pointing in different directions. After you lay it on the floor it will be clear if the floor is level, and if not, you will quickly see where leveling in needed. Although you might think you can get by with something "close" to level, over time those areas will begin to work apart. That rule holds with floating, glued, and nailed floors. There are numerous leveling products on the market and you would be well advised to use them to solve these potential problems before they rear their ugly heads.

Check For Square

The next step is important. It will effect the finished look of your entire floor. If you are going to install the wood the length of the room rather than across the room, take a tape and measure from one side to the other at about three or four points in the room. You want to find out how consistent the room is in its width. If, for example, at one end of the room, the measurement is 10'2" and at the other end of the room 10'4" you will need to make some adjustments.

If you start installing on one side of the room using a straight line that is perfectly parallel to the wall on that side, then when you reach the final installation stage on the other side of the room your line is 2" off and this will become a difficult issue as you complete the install of the room.

By finding that variable at the beginning of your installation, you can start your flooring on a line that is visually acceptable to traffic areas, leaving a rear corner or wall of the room to help hide the discrepancy. Plan ahead.

The Starting Line

Using our sample floor plan again as an example, we would recommend you start your first row on the long wall adjacent to the garage. Lay down a chalk line and begin your first row about ½ inch out from the wall **with the tongue of the wood facing away from the wall.** (This will leave a small space for expansion if needed).

Since a floor nailer is powerful enough to slightly move a board when it drives in the nail or staple, it is certainly acceptable to facenail or topnail the first row of boards to secure them before using your floor nailer. Be very careful that your first row stays right on the chalk line. If you start wrong, you'll finish wrong.

If you are installing a floating floor or click together product, it is wise to take the time to firmly establish your starting row. This can be done with a few small top nails that are not driven all the way into the wood underneath and can later be easily removed. Make a note to fill those small nail holes with an appropriate colored putty.

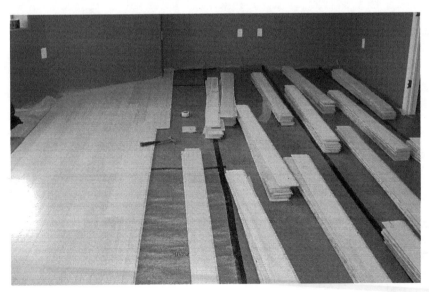

Laying out Bundles

Since nearly all boards in most pre-finished products come in long strips, laying out those strips in advance is for easy access to the variety of lengths that you will need as you move up and down the rows.

Startup & Setup Checklist

Door clearances   _____

Direction of wood   _____

Remove stool   _____

Remove pedestal sink   _____

Remove baseboard   _____

Remove old flooring   _____

Inspect the subfloor   _____

Check for level   _____

Check for square   _____

Start line   _____

Paper or Foam   _____

Laying out wood   _____

PART IV — INSTALLING

There are numerous ways you can choose to install your pre-finished flooring. We have included specific information on nail down, glue down, and floating installations. At the end of Part IV you will also find a handy Installation Checklist.

Compressor

Try to use a compressor that has accurate gauges. A compressor that is not adjustable can split edges and tongues making it difficult and time consuming.

Compressor pressure gauge and Nail Drive pressure gauge are important considerations when buying or renting any of the products on the market.

Nail Down Method — Using the Nailer

If you have selected a pre-finished product that you have chosen to nail into a wooden subfloor, then you should use one of the pneumatic nailers that are made for that installation. The thickness of your product will determine the length of the nail you should use for this installation.

For example, if you're installing a full ¾" strip pre-finished hardwood, load the nailer with 2" flooring nails. If you were shooting the nails straight down into the board you wouldn't use such a long nail, but since the flooring nailer shoots the nail at a substantial angle the 2" nail will give the floor good stability.

If you are installing over a wood subfloor that has pipes or radiant heat of some kind that is attached to beams under the subfloor and up tight against that subfloor, you will want to use a shorter nail.

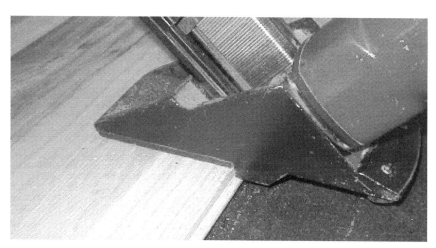

Notice how the ¼ " edge along the bottom of the nailer fits snugly into the groove above the tongue. This directs the nail through the top of the tongue at an angle to give the floor the stability it will need.

If you are installing over a wood subfloor that has pipes or radiant heat of some kind that is attached to beams under the subfloor and up tight against that subfloor, you will want to use a shorter nail.

It is important to test your nailer before starting your installation. To do this, connect your hose to the nailer and the compressor, and start the compressor to build pressure. There are adjustment knobs on the compressor that will let you control how high you want your pressure to build and rebuild during the installing process. Generally about 80-plus pounds is sufficient.

In the photo at the beginning of this chapter you can see the pressure to the nail gun has been set to maintain about 85 pounds. This needs to be set at a number that will drive the nail into the board far enough to be slightly below the surface of the board. If the nail head is not deep enough, the tongue and groove will not fit snugly on your next board. On the other hand, you don't want the nail to be countersunk so deeply that it splits the tongue. This adjustment can vary depending on the nailer and the species, but you might start at about 80 pounds as you test the nailer.

The photo illustrates how to set the nailer against the tongue side of the board, allowing the edge across the bottom of the nailer to fit snugly in the groove above the tongue. This allows the nail to shoot into the board at the top of the tongue and through the tongue into the subfloor at the desired angle.

That Critical First Row

Let me remind you (from page 18) — Using our sample floor plan again as an example, we would recommend you start your first row on the long wall adjacent to the garage. Lay down a chalk line and begin your first row about ½ inch out from the wall **with the tongue of the wood facing away from the wall.** (This will leave a small space for expansion if needed). This is one of the most important parts of your project. Time spent here will save a good deal of time and frustration later.

Remember as you start a row against one wall, the tongue should face the large open area of the room. This will be the direction you will be moving. As you start your rows near the wall, leave about ½ inch (follow the direction that came with your product) to give any wood room for some seasonal expansion. This gap needs to be covered by baseboard or quarter-round, so don't leave more gap than your trim will cover.

Ending The Rows

As a practical tip, set in a complete row before nailing. When you come to the end of each row, it will require that you cut a board to end the row. A nice shortcut to measuring for this is to spin the board around and mark it where it meets the end of the previous board (see following photo). This mark tells you exactly where to cut the board so that it will fit the space left in the row up to the ending wall.

Here is another tip: If the remainder of the board you just cut to finish the row at the ending wall is long enough, it can be used to start the next row at the starting wall since the end that is cut will go under your baseboard and on the other end you still end with a tongue.

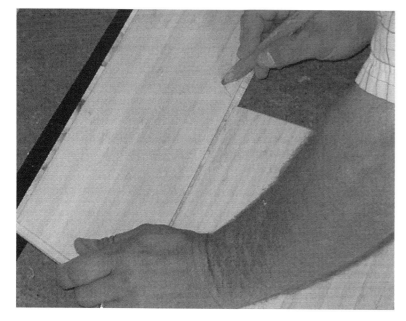

By turning the last board in a row so the groove faces the wall, you can mark where you want to cut the board with your chop saw. When you connect the board at the tongue and groove end, the cut end of the board is against the ending wall. This saves measuring and is usually more exact.

Watch Those End Joints

There are standards in the flooring industry that are wise to adhere to, so in laying out our flooring we select certain lengths of boards to run along previous rows making sure we stay in accord with those standards.

For example, in the first pictures (next page) we see what are called an "H's" and "Stair Steps." We do not want H's too close together. We don't want anything to call attention to the floor and any subtle pattern can be distracting. Always work to avoid those close end joints — even with another board between the two. Keep your end joints at least 6 inches, or more, from each other.

As you lay down a board, be sure you fully insert the groove onto the tongue of the previous board. Double check to avoid the H. Use the rubber end of an installing hammer or tapping block (next page) to tap the side of the board until it is fully up against the previous row. Then tap the open end of the new board to be sure the tongue and groove ends are tight.

23

 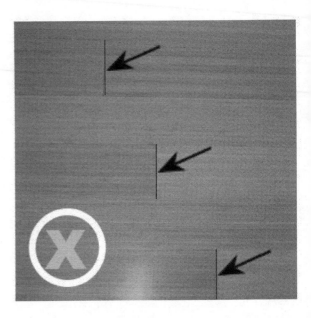

Even with a board in between you will notice an "H" (left). Always leave Hardwood • Vinyl • Laminate at least 6" from end joints that, when too close, become distracting. Also note the stair step effect (right) that is also distracting.

Tapping Blocks

Many manufacturers recommend, or provide, a tapping block that should be used to lightly tap the tongue into the groove of the preceding board. They are valuable and should always be used since the dried urethane coat on the surface of your boards can easily chip during installation — especially corners.

Many manufacturers have other products that perform the same function. It is always best to use the accessory and production products that are recommended by the flooring manufacturer.

Thresholds, Doors, Vents, Outlets

As you encounter other obstacles in your installation project, you will need other hand tools. For example, you will want to keep your jig saw near your table saw. The table saw gives you a nice table to lay or clamp a board as you make cuts for around door jambs, floor vents, floor electrical outlets, fixed thresholds, and other obstacles in your floor.

Putting a new blade in your jig saw will make the job easier. The species of wood you are installing will dictate, to some degree, how fine-toothed the blade should be for easy and accurate cutting.

Floating Method

If your installation method of choice is a floating floor you will be surpised at how easy the task is to complete, especially in light of the new click or snap together, or tongue and groove systems.

As with all other methods of installation, thoroughly read all of the specific manufacturer recommendations for installation to remain under their warranty guidelines. Most floating floor installations follow the same basic steps

Again referring back to "The Starting Line" in Part III, review the importance of laying out the first row. Just as a good carpenter measures twice and cuts once, we recommend you read that section again. This is one of the most important parts of your project. Time spent here will save a good deal of time and frustration later.

Remember as you start a row against one wall, the tongue should face the large open area of the room. This will be the direction you will be moving. As you start your rows near this wall, leave about ½ inch to give the wood room for any seasonal expansion. This gap needs to be covered by your baseboard or quarter-round, so be certain you don't leave more gap than your trim will cover.

Once you have established your starting line spread out your underlayment foam, or other recommended foam-type product, making certain to secure the edges together as the manuacturer suggested. The underlayment will serve as a moisture barrier as well as help to create a "quieter" sound from floor traffic.

Note in the photo how the underlayment is rolled out and also taped to assure stability plus full and complete coverage.

If possible lay out the underlayment so your starting line is visible, then put down a starter row using a piece of scrap wood or some of your flooring if you have plenty. Our procedure is to nail this row of scrap wood (even to concrete using concrete nails). This row will be used only as a solid, stable starting row and will be replaced later in the project.

With that solid row to work against, install your first row from end to end making certain all is going together correctly. From this point on, floating floors can install rather quickly especially in wide-open areas and rooms.

A Final Installation Note

When installing a floating floor, all of your transition pieces will connect to the flooring itself and never to the subfloor since we want the entire floor to float. This is necessary so the wood flooring can expand and contract seasonally as needed. Again, check carefully what your flooring manufacturer has to offer and what they recommend for a correct, stable installation.

Installation Checklist

Chop Saw   _____

Table Saw   _____

Jig Saw   _____

Rubber-end Hammer   _____

Nail Puller   _____

Pry Bar   _____

Glue   _____

Tapping Block   _____

Matching Putty   _____

Reminders

Measure first row twice   _____

Lay down starting line   _____

PART V — THE FINAL TOUCHES

Resetting the Trim

Installing your new hardwood flooring is an excellent time to clean up the base-boards in the project area. It will never be easier to work with then it is now. A fresh coat of paint or a new coat of stain and urethane will help to give the entire floor area a new and fresh look.

When resetting the baseboard, which has been numbered for its designated place on the wall, use your compressor and finish nailer. It is good to double-check your compressor settings to be sure the finish nailer lightly counter-sinks the nail, but doesn't drive it too deep into the baseboard. Most painted baseboard is pine and very soft, so it is possible to drive the nail all the way through the board. On the other hand, you want to be sure that your compressor is set to drive the nail deep enough to counter-sink it. When your project is complete you will go back and fill the counter-sunk holes with matching caulk or putty.

Be sure you press the base all the way down on the floor and all the way up against the wall before nailing. Shoot the nails into the upper half of the baseboard and into a stud if possible.

Installing Quarter Round

Using the same finish nailer, shoot the quarter round in under cabinets and other ar-eas that may need to have the edge of the flooring covered. Since quarter-round comes in more than one size, plan ahead. If you are going to leave about ½ inch be-tween the cabinet and the hardwood for expansion, then be sure you purchase a quarter-round that is ¾ inch.

Caulking

A good tip to remember when you get ready to caulk is how you cut the end of your caulking tube. It is common to just cut the end of the tube off anywhere to open it up for the caulk to squeeze out. But there is a better way to do that for this project.

Cut very near to the end of the tube nozzle (there are normally cut lines indicated on the plastic nozzle). Cut at an angle from the tip in. This is very important when you get to the phase of running a caulk bead across the top of the baseboard.

Run the caulking bead along the top of the baseboard using a very small opening on the end of the caulk tube.

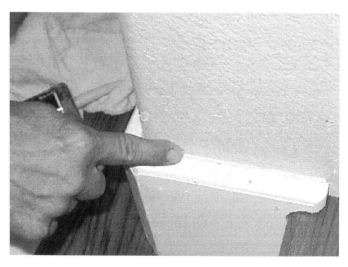

Wet your finger then run it very lightly along the bead of caulk giving a finished look to the baseboard.

Wet a household sponge, wring it out, and with your finger dab caulking (a color to match the wood finish) into the counter-sunk nail holes along the baseboard and/or quarter round. Lightly wipe the wet sponge across those areas to even out the caulk to a smooth look. As the caulk dries it may shrink slightly and leave a small dimple. This will become less noticeable as you reset the rooms with furniture, throw rugs, and items that draw attention away from tiny imperfections in all floors and trim.

Your final caulking step is to run a very thin bead of caulk along the top of the baseboard to conceal the small crack line between the baseboard and the wall.

Run the caulking bead a few feet in front of you or the complete length of that wall area. After you have run the small bead wet your finger slightly on the sponge and lightly run your finger along the length of the bead. This will even out the line of caulk, giving a smooth transition from baseboard to wall. If the caulk builds up against your finger wipe it on a rag and continue, going back over the line a second time. If it spreads beyond the bead line on to the baseboard or wall use the sponge to wipe it clean. Having a bucket of water handy can be helpful to keep the sponge clean and moist.

The Final Walk Through

Before calling your project complete we recommend you do a final walk through. Before you begin moving furniture, appliances, and other items back onto the floor, it is good to take a second look.

Carefully search for any residues of glue that you may have used in the process. Glue, once hardened, can be difficult to remove without marring the finish. Most manufacturers of flooring and glue products also have glue removers that work well with their products. When removing any glue spot be sure to completely remove all traces of the film it leaves.

Moving Back In - Very Carefully

Allow plenty of time for the floor to cure before moving furniture and appliances back into the rooms. Be very careful about setting heavy items on the finished product, especially items with a great deal of weight on a small leg or wheel. Setting a refrigerator down in front of its permanent space and then rolling it back into that space can leave roll marks or scratches in your new flooring. Even hardened urethane can be indented with tracks from heavy wheels.

Golf spikes and athletic cleats can leave marks, indentations, and scratches on your floors. Be careful that high heeled shoes are in good repair where the heel contacts the floor. Measured in pounds per square inch (psi), a car has a load of 28-30 psi, an elephant 50-100 psi, and a 125 pound woman with high heels 2,000 psi!

Throw rugs in entries, in front of the sink, refrigerator, and stove top are essentials to keeping your finish strong and durable. It is important to consider UV rays and their effect on your wood and finishes. If your rear entry door from a deck or patio is all glass and gets direct afternoon sun, it is important that you move, or roll up the throw rug in front of that door regularly so the sunlight that will bleach that area will bleach evenly and not create different shades of flooring under the throw rug and around that area.

Felt Pads

Always put felt pads on the bottom of chair and table legs. Most hardware stores sell both the nail in and stick-on types of pads.

It is also a good idea to occasionally turn the chairs over and, using an old toothbrush, lightly brush any dust and dirt particles that may be embedded in the pads. Chair legs carry a good deal of weight on them and the smallest grime can eventually cause surface scratching on your product finish.

Cleaning Your Floors

Do not use floor products on your floors that are not specifically recommended for hardwood floors and from known manufacturers. Using waxes, many oil-based cleaners, or vinyl and tile cleaners can cause floors to become slippery. These also dull their sheen and appearance over time. In addition, many of these products can prohibit a later maintenance coat from adhering correctly.

There are many good floor cleaning products on the market and available in most grocery and hardware stores.

We often hear that water and vinegar (four to one ratio) are good for cleaning hardwood, vinyl, and laminate floors. That is generally acceptable, however be careful to not pour water directly onto the floor and if you use a mop make sure that mop is only a damp mop or sponge. Your floors will expand in the more humid months and contract in the dry winter months. This contraction will develop small cracking in parts of the floor's surface, which will allow excess water to run into those small cracks.

Hardwood floor cleaning products should help you keep a visable sheen on your floor and keep it from becoming too dull.

Fillers and Cracking

Seasonal cracking is to be expected with hardwood flooring. Engineered flooring is substantially more stable and will have less movement with seasonal changes. If you have installed a full ¾ inch product however, as we have noted, cracks up to the width of a dime can be expected in the dry winter months as your hardwood loses much of its moisture content and shrinks.

Although hardwood fillers can be used to fill such cracks, it is advisable to let the wood move naturally during these periods. Filling those cracks in the dry months can result in the reverse problem in the humid months. As the hardwood takes on moisture again in spring and summer it expands, the small cracks close, and often the filler is pushed out and leaves you with filler edges along those cracks that can become even more noticeable.

Additional Information

For additional information about hardwood flooring, species, grades, installation, finishing, and maintenance, you can go to the following website:

National Wood Flooring Association (NWFA)

https://www.nwfa.org

Notes

Made in the USA
Las Vegas, NV
13 September 2023

77528200R00020